A Likkle Miss Lou

In the loving memory of my younger brother, Roury Hohn, a true roots man who had a deep
love for Jamaica, and my first publisher, Sheila Barry, who believed in me and in this book
—N.L.H.

For Stephanie Martin,
who gave me the rhythm of the words
—E.F.

Text © 2019 Nadia L. Hohn | Illustrations © 2019 Eugenie Fernandes

All works by Louise Bennett Coverley are © Louise Bennett Coverley Estate (LBCE) and permission
for their use has been granted by Coverley Holdings Inc. for LBCE by Co-Executors Judge Pamela
Appelt (pappelt14@gmail.com) and Fabian Coverley, B.Th. (fcoverley@gmail.com).

Photo of Louise Bennett Coverley courtesy of McMaster University Library.
Used with the permission of the Louise Bennett Coverley Estate.

Owlkids Books acknowledges the financial support of the Canada Council for the Arts,
the Ontario Arts Council, the Government of Canada through the Canada Book Fund (CBF)
and the Government of Ontario through the Ontario Creates Book Initiative
for our publishing activities.

Published in Canada by Owlkids Books Inc., 1 Eglinton Avenue East, Toronto, ON M4P 3A1
Published in the US by Owlkids Books Inc., 1700 Fourth Street, Berkeley, CA 94710

Library of Congress Control Number: 2018963956

Library and Archives Canada Cataloguing in Publication

Hohn, Nadia L., author
A likkle Miss Lou : how Jamaican poet Louise Bennett
Coverley found her voice / written by Nadia L. Hohn ; illustrated
by Eugenie Fernandes.

ISBN 978-1-77147-350-7 (hardcover)

1. Bennett, Louise, 1919-2006--Juvenile fiction.
I. Fernandes, Eugenie, 1943-, illustrator II. Title. III. Title: How
Jamaican poet Louise Bennett Coverley found her voice.

PS8615.O396L55 2019   jC813'.6   C2018-906581-8

Edited by Karen Li | Designed by Alisa Baldwin

Manufactured in Shenzhen, Guangdong, China, in March 2019, by C&C Offset
Job #HT1208

A   B   C   D   E   F

A Likkle Miss Lou

HOW JAMAICAN POET
LOUISE BENNETT COVERLEY
FOUND HER VOICE

Written by
Nadia L. Hohn

Illustrated by
Eugenie Fernandes

Owlkids Books

Louise Bennett loved words. She played with them. She ate them up for breakfast, served with roasted breadfruit, ackee, and saltfish. She swallowed each word whole.

When it came to speaking, Louise's words got stuck in her throat. But she found a way to unlock them. Her pen was the key and her notebook the door.

At school, Louise's teacher thought that words had to click like clacking wheels, and that sentences should line up like the tramcar tracks in Kingston. Louise got good grades, but she wanted more.

A

May 1, 1928

'I wish' I wished, 'that I could be
A poet great and with my pen
Trace paths of peace and harmony
For the uncertain minds of men.'

Louise

Each day, she passed the men working on the Kingston streets, weary and glistening in the broiling heat. They heaved and huffed, filling the sides of the dirt road in a rhythm.

Hill an gully rider
Hill an gully
Hill an gully rider
Hill an gully
An I bend dung low dung
Hill an gully
An I bend dung low dung
Hill an gully

At school, Louise tried to find the **bend dung low dung** of the men's shovels. She wanted to hear their songs on the paper, the bass in her pen, the drum from their words.

Louise was lost in her thoughts, wondering what voice she should listen to. The one with words that lined up like schoolgirls in starched uniforms? Or the other voice?

"Louise Bennett!" her teacher called.

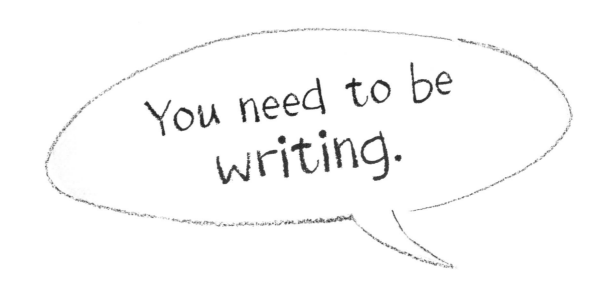

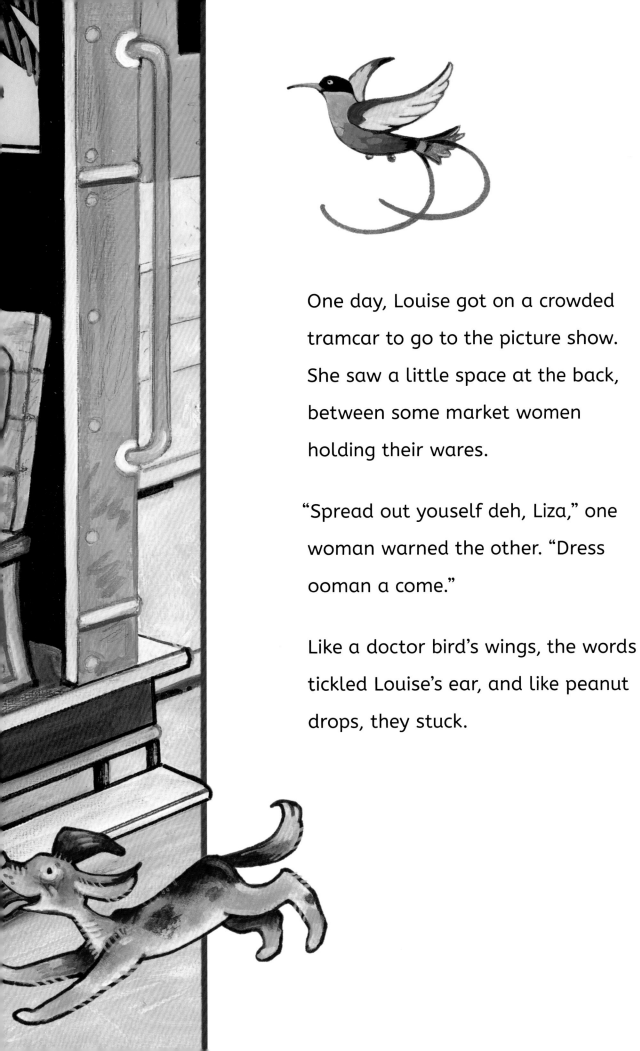

One day, Louise got on a crowded tramcar to go to the picture show. She saw a little space at the back, between some market women holding their wares.

"Spread out youself deh, Liza," one woman warned the other. "Dress ooman a come."

Like a doctor bird's wings, the words tickled Louise's ear, and like peanut drops, they stuck.

That evening, Louise sat down to do her homework. The special words snuck into the margins of her notebook pages. Something smart. Something clever.

"What's this?" her teacher asked in class the next morning. "This is not fit for a top school. It is certainly not why your mother sent you here."

At home, as her mother worked, Louise watched the peel head John Crows sitting in the treetops. They reminded her of the stories she heard during visits to her grandmother in Saint Mary. Louise had listened to the countrypeople singing:

Elena and her mumma go a grung
Elena start bawl fe har belly.

Louise held her stomach, too, remembering her day at school.

"Everyting aright, Bibsie," said Mummy as she moved the cloth under the sewing machine's darting needle, stitching the fabric together.

sousou

tallawah

boonoonoonoos

pickney

bangarang

mi soon com

bankra

That night, Louise heard the door creak open and clang shut.
The teacher lady was leaving as the higgler lady came in.
Their words danced through the walls lively, and Louise's ears
  perked up.

"Good evening, Mrs. Robinson. I must say I love this silhouette."

"Come here, mah … Naw, miss, de frock fit you nice."

"Mrs. Robinson, you have outdone yourself once again."

"A dat style wearin' now."

Louise drifted off to the rhythm of Mummy's heeled shoe
hitting the tiled floor and lifting the pedal.

"Get all your things, Bibs," her mother said the next day. "You're going to a new school."

Louise was shocked. But when she looked at the name of her new school, she loved it immediately. E-X-C-E-L-S-I-O-R. The letters tasted like the crisp water crackers she loved to eat with Mummy's thick Saturday punkin soup.

September 12, 1928

It was a warm September day.
Along North Street I made my way.
I stopped at the gate and heaved a sigh.
One word caught my eye:

Excelsior!

At Louise's new school, teachers encouraged students to memorize poems. Then on Friday afternoons, they recited them aloud.

Louise thought of speaking in front of her new friends and teachers, and she panicked—the words lodged in her throat again.

When it was finally her turn, Louise remembered the ladies on the bus. They were funny and chatty, bold and confident. She opened her mouth:

'Pread out yuself deh, Liza.
Dress ooman a come.
She see de lil' space side a wi
and waan poke herself in deh.
Spread out, gal, she da come.
No space in yah at all!
Wha mek yu fool so, Liza?
'Pread out yuself, nuh gal.

Louise waited. Did her classmates hate it? Would they think she didn't know how to "talk right"? Would her new teacher scold her?

Instead, her classmates roared with laughter and clapped. Her teacher, Mr. Powell, even smiled. Everyone begged her to recite more, and she did— a new poem every week.

Louise had finally found a safe place to share her beloved words.

And one day she would take them to the world.

A Note from the Author

During one of Louise's performances, the playwright Eric "Chalk Talk" Coverley sat in the audience. A friend had shown him some of Louise's poetry, and he'd liked it right away. At the end of the show, Louise won a book for Outstanding Literary Talent. She asked Mr. Chalk Talk to sign it. "Great success to you. You possess an unusual talent. Develop it," he wrote.

It took a few tries, but Eric convinced Louise to perform her poetry at the Christmas party at Coke Methodist Church in 1936. Everyone laughed and enjoyed the performance—and Louise was paid enough to buy a new pair of shoes.

Louise's dialect poems sounded like the speech of everyday Jamaicans—poor and rich, light and dark. They sounded the way that her grandmother spoke. Even the ladies who spoke their careful words in "proper English" knew how to speak in Jamaican patois, which is another word for Jamaican English.

Louise submitted her poems to the *Daily Gleaner* newspaper, where they were at first rejected. But she kept sending new ones. And when one was published months later, it was an instant hit!

My introduction to Louise Bennett Coverley was in a library book called *Mango Spice: 44 Caribbean Songs* and its accompanying tape recording. These materials were filled with Jamaican folk songs arranged or written by Miss Lou, as well as music from other Caribbean islands. My younger sister and I were children at the time, and we were so excited to find a book that reflected our culture and sounded the way we spoke at home.

We memorized the songs as I fumbled their melodies on the piano. Hearing our efforts jogged the memories of our parents, who had immigrated to Canada from Jamaica in the early 1970s. With smiles on their faces, they told us of Miss Lou and her radio show, which they had listened to as children.

Born in Kingston, Jamaica, on September 7, 1919, Louise Bennett Coverley was raised by her mother, Kerene Robinson, a dressmaker, after her father, Augustus Cornelius Bennett, passed away. After her time at Excelsior College, Louise decided to get more formal training in drama. She was offered a scholarship to the Royal Academy of Dramatic Art in London, England, in 1945. She was the first Black student. She was also the first Black person to host a radio show on the BBC, a British radio network that broadcasts its programs around the world.

Louise Bennett Coverley's impact has been felt throughout the Caribbean diaspora and the world. She shared the mento folk songs, proverbs, and stories of Jamaica in her books and in her performances on stage, on the radio, and on *Ring Ding*, a children's television show. She married Eric "Chalk Talk" Coverley in 1954, and they worked together on many projects. Louise and Eric raised his son, Fabian, and adopted other children. Louise lived in Jamaica, the United Kingdom, and the United States, and she spent the last twenty years of her life in Canada, where she died in 2006.

I would have loved to meet Miss Lou. Like her, I am a teacher, an author, and a budding playwright, and I love to sing and perform Caribbean folk songs dressed in traditional costumes. Miss Lou performed in Jamaican English at a time when speaking the language was discouraged. Thanks to her, patois was embraced internationally, and she created spaces for poets like Mutabaruka and Linton Kwesi Johnson, and singers like Bob Marley and Harry Belafonte. My first picture books, *Malaika's Costume* and *Malaika's Winter Carnival*, are written in both standard English and Caribbean patois. We owe all of this to Miss Lou.

Thank you, Miss Lou, for the many gifts you have given to this world, and for being a phenomenal woman. In your words, may we all "walk good."

GLOSSARY

ACKEE: A red fruit originally from West Africa. Its yellow insides taste like scrambled eggs.

BAWL: A crying complaint.

BREADFRUIT: A greenish-brown Caribbean fruit, originally from Tahiti. Its whitish/brownish starchy insides, eaten cooked, taste like bread.

DOCTOR BIRD: Jamaica's national bird. A species of hummingbird.

GO A GRUNG: Go into the fields to work or plant.

HIGGLER: In Jamaica or the West Indies, someone who sells small items wherever possible.

LIKKLE: Little.

PEANUT DROPS: A Jamaican sweet made with ginger, molasses, and peanuts. Similar to peanut brittle.

PEEL HEAD JOHN CROW: A Jamaican nickname for a bird that eats dead or rotting flesh—for example, a buzzard.

SALTFISH: Salted codfish, originally from Newfoundland. Part of Jamaica's national dish of ackee and saltfish.

TRAMCAR: A mode of transportation used in cities. A single car that runs on tracks.

WARES: Various items for sale.

WATER CRACKER: A hard biscuit made from baked flour and water. Excelsior is a popular brand of water cracker in Jamaica.

REFERENCES

PAGE 6: "'I wish' I wished, 'that I could be …'" is an unpublished poem cited in the introduction to *Selected Poems: Louise Bennett* by Louise Bennett, edited by Mervyn Morris (Kingston, Jamaica: Sangster's Book Stores Limited, 1982).

PAGE 8: "Hill an Gully Rider" is a traditional Jamaican folk song.

PAGE 16: "Louise watched the peel head John Crows sitting in the treetops" is a reference to the lyrics for "Dis Long Time Gal," a traditional Jamaican folk song.

PAGE 16: "Elena and her mumma go a grung …" is from "Cerasee," a traditional Jamaican folk song.

PAGE 20: "It was a warm September day …" is from an unpublished source cited in *Recalling Recitation in the Americas: Borderless Curriculum, Performance Poetry, and Reading* by Janet Neigh (Toronto: University of Toronto Press, 2017).

PAGE 24: "On a Tramcar" is from *(Jamaica) Dialect Verses* by Louise Bennett, edited by George R. Bowen (Kingston, Jamaica: Herald Ltd., 1942). Used by permission of Louise Bennett Coverley Estate (LBCE).

PAGE 29: *Mango Spice: 44 Caribbean Songs*, chosen by Yvonne Conolly, Gloria Cameron, and Sonia Singham; with music arranged by Chris Cameron and Vallin Miller; and with drawings by Maggie Ling (London: A&C Black, 1981).